Cryp

Why Christians Must Not Participate

Dr. June Dawn Knight

Dr. June Dawn Knight

Treehouse Publishers
www.treehousepublishers.com
Printed in the United States of America

Copyright © 2022 Dr. June Dawn Knight
All rights reserved.
ISBN: 9798444089880

DEDICATION

I dedicate this book to the last day Bride. We are going to make some tough decisions in the coming days and I pray God's grace be with you all.

Crypto & Bitcoin – Why Christians Must Not Participate
@2022 Dr. June Dawn Knight
8th Book in the *What the World?* Series

All rights reserved. No part of this book may be copied or reproduced in any form, whether electronic, mechanical, photocopying, recordings, and otherwise without written permission from the author or publisher.

CONTENTS

1	What is the Digital Money?	Pg. 01
2	Government Notes	Pg. 21
3	Scriptural Basis About Digital Money in End-Time Scenario	Pg. 87
	About Author	Pg. 103

Christmas 2019 after I left White House

Preface to this Book:

Bride, I want to say that I am not an economist or specialist in money. My intentions are not to explain it all in a scientific manner. If I miss it here and there about the science of it, please forgive me. My goal in this book is to merely introduce you to the basic concepts of what they're doing. My goal is more to show you the connection to the Beast through this technology. Thank you and I pray that I am successful in this mission.

Dr. June Dawn Knight

1
What is the Digital Money?

Most of us grew up in a society based on cash. We had banks, but most families kept their money at home in jars or hidden in the walls. We finally grew to where we trusted banks to hold our cash. Over the years we began to use credit cards and our smart phones to make purchases. Now we are gradually transitioning to all digital. With COVID-19 agenda, they are using this situation to switch it over to digital only by easing fears of "touching other people's money." They want to do away with physical contact and go to six-feet distance, digital conversations, and digital money. Basically, they want everything fake and synthetic.

As we learn about digital money, let's learn some definitions first:

- **ATM Network** - Asynchronous Transfer Mode (ATM) is a cell-switching, connection-oriented technology. In ATM networks, end stations attach to the network using dedicated full duplex connections. The ATM networks are constructed using switches, and switches are interconnected using dedicated physical connections. Before any data transfers can begin, end-to-end connections must be established. Multiple connections can and do exist on a single physical interface.[1]

- **Biometric Technology** - Biometric technologies generally refer to **the use of technology to identify a person based on some aspect of their biology**. Fingerprint recognition is one of the first and original biometric technologies that have been grouped loosely under digital forensics.[2]

- **Biometric Trait** - In the future, other biometrics from emerging modalities, including 3D face, DNA, gait and electrocardiogram, show potential as a means of connecting the digital and physical world and enabling a secure and seamless traveler journey[3]

- **Bioinformatics Platform** - The goal of the bioinformatics platform is to provide highly-specialized bioinformatics support in the areas of genomics, epigenomics, transcriptomics, proteomics, high-throughput screen deconvolution and systems biology.[4]

- **Blockchain** - A blockchain is a distributed database that is shared among the nodes of a computer network. As a database, a blockchain stores information electronically in digital format. Blockchains are best known for their crucial role in cryptocurrency systems, such as Bitcoin, for maintaining a

---

[1] https://www.ibm.com/docs/en/aix/7.1?topic=adapters-atm-technology

[2] https://www.sciencedirect.com/topics/computer-science/biometric-technology#:~:text=Biometric%20technologies%20generally%20refer%20to,grouped%20loosely%20under%20digital%20forensics

[4] https://ki.se/en/research/bioinformatics-platform

secure and decentralized record of transactions. The innovation with a blockchain is that it guarantees the fidelity and security of a record of data and generates trust without the need for a trusted third party[5]

- **Cryptology** – CIA uses this to talk to one another? Cryptology.com describes it as, "Cryptology is a digital asset trading platform with the ability to trade futures contracts with up to x100 leverage, with spot trading, bank card support, and some of the lowest fees on the market."[6]

- **Crypto-currency** - Cryptocurrency, sometimes called crypto-currency or crypto, is **any form of currency that exists digitally or virtually and uses cryptography to secure transactions**. Cryptocurrencies don't have a central issuing or regulating authority, instead using a decentralized system to record transactions and issue new units.[7]

- **Cryptography** - Cryptography is an indispensable tool for protecting information in computer systems. In this course you will learn the inner workings of cryptographic systems and how to correctly use them in real-world applications.[8]

- **Data** - facts and statistics collected together for reference or analysis.

---
[5] https://www.investopedia.com/terms/b/blockchain.asp
[6] https://cryptology.com/
[7] https://www.kaspersky.com/resource-center/definitions/what-is-cryptocurrency
[8] https://www.coursera.org/learn/crypto

- **Data Nodes** - A node is any physical device within a network of other tools that's able to send, receive, or forward information. A personal computer is the most common node. It's called the computer node or internet node.[9]
- **Decentralized System vs. Centralized System** - In centralization, the higher positions of the management hold the decision-making authority. Further, in decentralization, the management disperses the decision-making authority across the organization and brings it closer to the source of action and information.[10]
- **Digital ID System** - hey make sure everyone has a way of verifying their identity to transact with the public and private sectors online. This simple feature has profound implications for every country's digital transformation journey, as well as its development goals. More than a billion people around the world have no formal way of proving who they are. In many instances, this leads to struggles in securing basic government services, including access to public healthcare, education, voting services and benefit programs. A digital identity will make these services more accessible, while improving quality of life for locals.[11]

---

[9] https://www.lifewire.com/what-is-a-node-4155598
[10] https://www.toppr.com/guides/business-management-and-entrepreneurship/organizing/centralization-and-decentralization/
[11] https://www.forbes.com/sites/jumio/2021/05/03/how-national-digital-ids-benefit-both-citizens-and-businesses/?sh=6aa102696fc6

- **Distributed Ledger Technology** - DLT is a decentralized database managed by multiple participants, across multiple nodes. Blockchain is a type of DLT where transactions are recorded with an immutable cryptographic signature called a hash. The transactions are then grouped in blocks and each new block includes a hash of the previous one, chaining them together, hence why distributed ledgers are often called blockchains.[12]
- **Equity** – The word equity is defined as "**the quality of being fair or impartial; fairness; impartiality**" or "something that is fair and just." Equity also has several meanings related to finance and property law that aren't relevant for our discussion. The adjective form of equity is equitable.[13]
- **FIDO-certified application** - FIDO's certification programs are a critical element in ensuring an interoperable ecosystem of products and services that organizations can leverage to deploy FIDO Authentication solutions worldwide. FIDO Alliance manages functional certification programs for its core specifications (UAF, U2F and FIDO2) to validate product conformance and interoperability, and in addition has introduced programs to delineate security capabilities of FIDO Certified Authenticators as well as to test and validate the efficacy of biometric components.[14]

---

[12] https://www.r3.com/blockchain-101/
[13] https://www.dictionary.com/e/equality-vs-equity/
[14] https://fidoalliance.org/certification/

- Fourth Industrial Revolution - The 4th Industrial Revolution (4IR) is a fusion of advances in artificial intelligence (AI), robotics, the Internet of Things (IoT), genetic engineering, quantum computing, and more. **What exactly is the Fourth Industrial Revolution — and why should you care?** The Fourth Industrial Revolution is a way of describing the blurring of boundaries between the physical, digital, and biological worlds. It's a fusion of advances in artificial intelligence (AI), robotics, the Internet of Things (IoT), 3D printing, genetic engineering, quantum computing, and other technologies. It's the collective force behind many products and services that are fast becoming indispensable to modern life. Think GPS systems that suggest the fastest route to a destination, voice-activated virtual assistants such as Apple's Siri, personalized Netflix recommendations, and Facebook's ability to recognize your face and tag you in a friend's photo.[15]
- **Hubs** – A hub may refer to any of the following: When referring to a network, a hub is the most basic networking device that connects multiple computers or other network devices together.[16]
    - **Global Hubs** – You will see hubs in almost every city. One of the main indicators is that it has a circle. **O**

---

[15] https://www.salesforce.com/blog/what-is-the-fourth-industrial-revolution-4ir/
[16] https://www.computerhope.com/jargon/h/hub.htm

- **IATA's One ID Initiative** - IATA's One ID initiative seeks to introduce a streamlined, friction-free and passenger-centric process that allows an individual to assert their identity, online or in person, to the required level at every process step in the end-to-end passenger journey, while maintaining the privacy of personal data. The concept relies on a single capture and controlled distribution of passenger data among the various stakeholders on an authorized-to-know basis. If a passenger's identity can be confirmed at every touchpoint, it will become easier to deliver a more personalized customer experience, while enabling significant improvements in operational efficiency and security. To achieve this, true collaboration between stakeholders will be paramount.[17]

- **Incentivizing Mechanism** - A means of providing blockchain network users an award for activities within the blockchain network (typically used as a system to reward successful publishing of blocks).[18]

- **Mobile Interface** - A mobile user interface (mobile UI) is the graphical and usually touch-sensitive display on a mobile device, such as a smartphone or tablet, that allows the user to interact with the device's apps, features, content and functions.[19]

---

[17] https://www3.weforum.org/docs/WEF_The_Known_Traveller_Digital_Identity_Concept.pdf

[18] https://csrc.nist.gov/glossary/term/incentive_mechanism#:~:text=A%20means%20of%20providing%20blockchain,reward%20successful%20publishing%20of%20blocks).

[19] https://www.techtarget.com/searchmobilecomputing/definition/mobile-UI-mobile-user-interface#:~:text=A%20mobile%20user%20interface%20(mobile,%2C%20features%2C%20content%20and%20functions

- **Peer-to-Peer Transactions** - Peer-to-peer payment services let you use a bank account or a credit or debit card to pay friends or family from your phone.[20]

- **Petro-Dollar** - Petrodollars are U.S. dollars paid to an oil-exporting country. Petrodollars are the primary source of revenue for many OPEC members and other oil exporters. Oil exporters settle sales in U.S. dollars because the dollar is the most widely used currency, making it easier for them to invest export proceeds.[21]

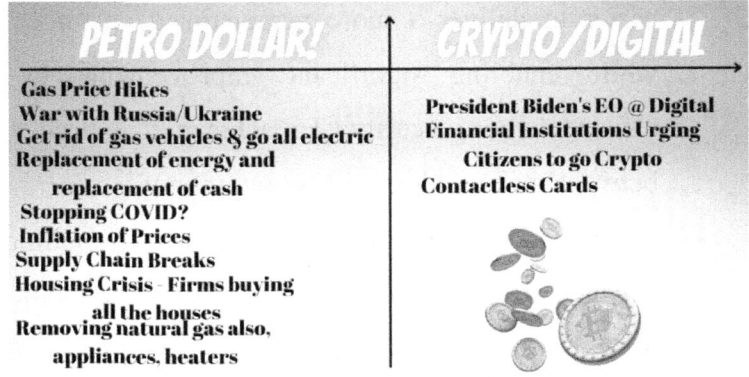

- **Public/Private Key** – The most commonly used implementations of public key cryptography (also known as public-key encryption and asymmetric encryption) are based on algorithms presented by Rivest-Shamir-Adelman (RSA) Data Security. Public key cryptography involves a pair of keys known as a public key and a private key (a *public key pair*),

---

[20] https://www.nerdwallet.com/article/banking/p2p-payment-systems
[21] https://www.investopedia.com/terms/p/petrodollars.asp#:~:text=Petrodollars%20are%20U.S.%20dollars%20paid,them%20to%20invest%20export%20proceeds

which are associated with an entity that needs to authenticate its identity electronically or to sign or encrypt data. Each public key is published and the corresponding private key is kept secret. Data that is encrypted with the public key can be decrypted only with the corresponding private key.'[22]

- **RFID** – Radio frequency identification device. This is a computer chip that will read the frequencies.
- **Transparency** - Transparency in business is the basis for trust between a firm and its investors, customers, partners, and employees. Being transparent means being honest and open when communicating with stakeholders about matters related to the business.[23]

WORLD ECONOMIC FORUM DESCRIPTION OF DIGITAL ECONOMY

This is the Fourth Industrial Revolution, and it's going to have a massive impact on the economy as well. Already we're seeing the rise of the sharing economy, blockchain technology, and changes in manufacturing driven by 3D- and 4D-printing.

The sharing economy is a model in which people and organizations connect online to share goods and services. It is also known as collaborative consumption or peer-to-peer exchange. Two of the best-known examples of the sharing economy are Uber (transportation) and Airbnb (housing).

---

[22] https://www.ibm.com/docs/en/ztpf/1.1.0.15?topic=concepts-public-key-cryptography
[23] https://www.ganintegrity.com/compliance-glossary/transparency-in-business/

Blockchain is a digital "ledger" technology that allows for keeping track of transactions in a distributed and trusted fashion. It replaces the need for third-party institutions to provide trust for financial, contract, and voting activities. Bitcoin and other digital currencies are some of the most well-known examples of applications of blockchain technology.[24]

On the weforum.org website, you will notice they have the whole plan of the Great Reset (global one world order) laid out for anyone to examine. You need to check it out Bride.

Thus, if I could explain how the World Economic Forum (brain of the Beast) is planning with the digital economy it would be like this....

The fourth industrial revolution is the globe coming together to merge like a machine. The revolution is the synchronization of everything. It is like the black goo you see on videos where it all meshes together. They are coming together to form their big tower of babel to form a utopia of Lucifer's world. This world is synthetic and fake – just like the digital money. However, in order for you to participate in this world, you must have the main ingredient – the vaccine. Why? Because it will connect the app on the inside of you and insert the little robots that will be at the Beast's bidding to build back better.

---

[24] https://www.weforum.org/agenda/2016/11/the-digital-economy-what-is-it-and-how-will-it-transform-our-lives/

Their build back better agenda is to build the human better as well. I just read an article the other day about these nanobots working to build the human to where one day there will be no disease, etc. It's like the marvel movies where they fill the children and families with ideas of super-powers. This new world they're building will be a world similar to that.

So, once you have the app, it's going to contain the digital wallet, etc., that will be your bank. In this plan, the digital wallet will be on the inside of you.

Internet of DNA - It refers to a global network of millions of sequenced genomes which can be medicine's next great advance for disease diagnosis and treatment. Up to date, more than 200,000 people have already had their genomes sequenced and this continues to rise.[25]

Capital One, one of the biggest banks, describes the digital wallet, "Digital wallets are exactly what they sound like. They're electronic versions of your physical wallet. They can store things like credit card information, loyalty cards and even tickets you've purchased.

You can access that personal data from devices like your smartphone, smartwatch, computer or tablet. This can help you declutter and avoid carrying a bunch of physical cards around with you. And it can make payments quick and easy.

---

[25] https://www.enzolifesciences.com/science-center/technotes/2015/march/internet-of-dna/#:~:text=Internet%20of%20DNA!,and%20this%20continues%20to%20rise

What's the Difference Between Digital Wallets and Mobile Wallets?

The terms "digital wallet" and "mobile wallet" are often used interchangeably. But they can also refer to slightly different things.

Basically, "digital wallet" is an umbrella term that includes mobile wallets.

A digital wallet is software that stores your payment information and can be installed on your desktop computer, laptop or mobile device.[26]

WHAT IS BLOCKCHAIN?

Blockchain is like building blocks of data. Each group of data is a box and they link together in a chain. It's like a DNA helix.

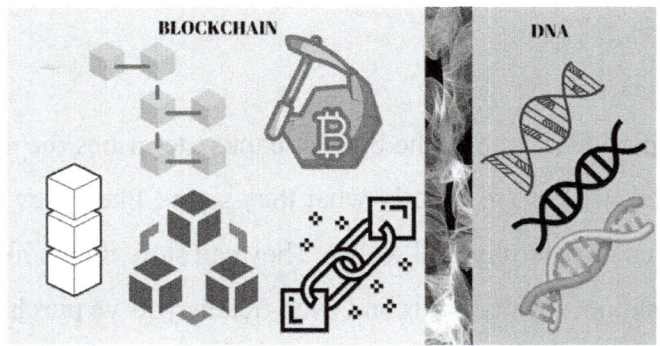

- o It is a shared database that is kept in blocks of data. It is then linked together by cryptography.
- o New data equals new block. Once it is filled with data, it is then connected to previous block in chronological order.
- o The ledgers mostly contain transactions.

---

[26] https://www.capitalone.com/learn-grow/money-management/mobile-wallet/

- Different types of data can be contained within same block
- With Bitcoin, the blockchain is decentralized so that all users retain control – the collective ownership.
- Once data enters in, it is irreversible. They are permanently recorded and viewable to anyone.

Blockchain defined: Blockchain is a shared, immutable ledger that facilitates the process of recording transactions and tracking assets in a business network. An asset can be tangible (a house, car, cash, land) or intangible (intellectual property, patents, copyrights, branding). Virtually anything of value can be tracked and traded on a blockchain network, reducing risk and cutting costs for all involved.[27]

I think you pretty much get the point now. Here's another analogy. The Beast eats your data like dinner and keeps it in its memory bank (brain) to use against you at any time.

So let's examine how this is working with these video platforms:

Odysee Video Platform Example

Lately YouTube and Vimeo platforms are not allowing me upload videos due to my controversial content (vaccine agenda, global world order, etc.). I know not to trust iConnect or BitChute. I was reading the Terms of Service for this platform and look at this:

---

[27] https://www.ibm.com/topics/what-is-blockchain

This section applies if you use the Services to publish Content through Odysee. a) You will make available via the Services a clear and accurate description of Content you publish, and provide the Content in accordance with any descriptions or representations you make available about the Content. You are solely responsible for resolving any disputes with users of your Content, including any chargebacks or refunds, and for any and all injuries, illnesses, damages, claims, liabilities and costs that are caused in whole or in part by you or your Content. **Publishing to a blockchain is permanent.** We cannot remove published content from the blockchain itself, although we can block content accessed via our app or other services on **top of the blockchain.**[28]

In the beginning of their TOS they mention they are a decentralized platform. That told me they were involved with the Circular Economy. Notice how they say that "publishing to a blockchain is permanent", this means that your data you now provide is forever recorded in a block.

This is the BUILD BACK BETTER agenda. Picture to the left is what a blockchain looks like.

---

[28] https://odysee.com/$/tos

Targeting the Children through Video Games

I think about my grandson who plays that game Minecraft. The whole point of the game is to build blocks. The whole purpose of the show is to learn how to build like data mining. They mine through blocks to get the jewels (which we know is crypto-currency). God help us!

According to their website, "Prepare for an adventure of limitless possibilities as you build, mine, battle mobs, and explore the ever-changing Minecraft landscape."[29] Notice how it says "mine". This is data mining. Children are playing this game from five years old and up. It is teaching children how to build in the Metaverse. Microsoft bought it in 2014 for billions of dollars and it is the #1 video game of all time.

Here is a visual to it:

___

[29] https://www.minecraft.net/en-us/about-minecraft

Going back to Video Platforms

BitChute – This video platform is just how it sounds. It is taking your data and shooting it down the file chute. It is sucking your data. It is a lot like the GETTR logo that we examined one night. It contains a data mining tool and sucking down the Twitter bird. According to BITchute's own Terms of Service, "Welcome to BitChute, a peer-to-peer content sharing platform and associated services (collectively known as the "Service")."[30]

What is a peer-to-peer content sharing platform? It is just like it sounds. It is where the data is shared through computers and devices via this software. Watch this, "Peer-to-peer (P2P) file sharing is the distribution of digital media such as software, videos, music, and images through an informal network in order to upload and download files. Typically, P2P software allows users to select which files to share. These files are indexed on a central server, making them available for other users to find and download. Sharing media is not illegal if you have the right to distribute the content. However, many file sharing applications are used to illegally access copyrighted material."[31]

Basically, it is giving the Beast all of the data on your computers and devices.

iConnect – is basically the same type of service. It is a file-sharing program. Very invasive.

---

[30] https://support.bitchute.com/policy/terms/
[31] https://www.it.northwestern.edu/security/illegaldownloading/index.html

Where are we headed? Well, if YouTube does not like my video content, I cannot upload on another platform once being on YouTube because now that data is in the chain somewhere. I have this very thing happening right now. YouTube does not want the data on their site and neither does Vimeo. So, if I was to acquire a service myself or host the files myself, it will not matter in the coming days. The AI Beast will scan that video and will reject the upload/content. Can you see how they are going to control what is online in the near future?

Arguments that it's not Tied to the Mark of the Beast

I saw this opinion on a website and thought how I've heard this many times before. People defend Crypto currency by proclaiming it's for "we the people" and does away with banks, global governance, and the people have control of it. This is the furthest from the truth. However, here is a random opinion:

Some people are arguing that Bitcoin will be the currency for the Mark of the Beast. I want to say a few things to get rid of this myth.

This interpretation is literalistic (and literalism does not work well for Revelation). And is putting a very 21st Century interpretation on a document written in the first Century.

Bitcoin is very resistant to becoming a One World Gov currency. Bitcoin by nature is censorship resistant. This means Bitcoin allows me to:

1. Store it on any wallet I choose.

2. Send it to any address I choose without asking a governmental authority for permission (see banks).

3. Send it anytime I choose. You don't even need an internet connection to send Bitcoin you can do it with a HAM Radio or a Bitcoin satellite connection!

So please tell me how a government can force everyone to use Bitcoin with a chip in their head? Bitcoin does not care how the Satoshi's are sent! It's also pseudonymous which means the government has to figure out who owns the Bitcoin address before they can really track you.

If you want to see a mark of the beast currency it won't be Bitcoin. It would be more likely to be the US Dollar or Facebook's Libra coin (they will track all of your purchases). If you want to opt out of government-controlled currency Bitcoin is your friend not your enemy.[32]

My Answer:

If this man thinks that the governments will not have access to the blocks, then he's very misinformed. Who does he think is the AI? The AI is the beast. The artificial intelligence is like a Beast feeding off all the date it is receiving. I've shared on these *What the World* books that it is like a spider. The body of the spider (fat part) is the data, the UN and governing body is like the head and the mesh (global internet mesh) is like the spider web that is spun by the legs of the spider. Let me insert some of the pictures.

---

[32] https://www.quora.com/Where-in-the-Bible-does-it-talk-about-cryptocurrency

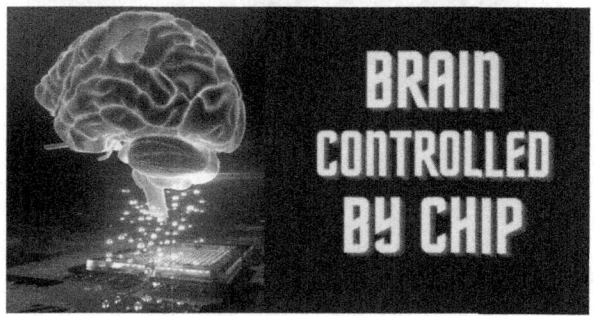

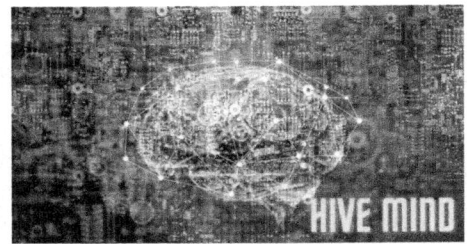

hive mind
1. a notional entity consisting of a large number of people who share their knowledge or opinions with one another, regarded as producing either uncritical conformity or collective intelligence.
2. "he has become one of those celebrities whose online presence has made him a favorite of the internet hive mind"
   - (in science fiction) a unified consciousness or intelligence formed by a number of alien individuals, the resulting consciousness typically exerting control over its constituent members.
   - "there is a Borg Queen who controls the hive mind"

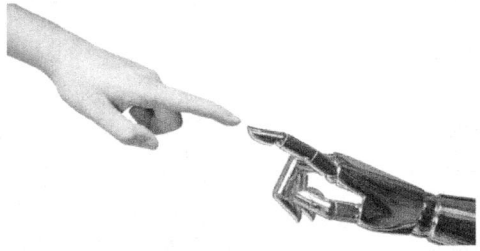

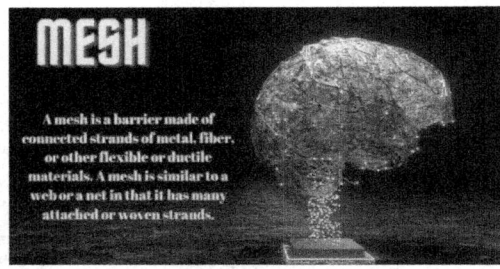

MESH

A mesh is a barrier made of connected strands of metal, fiber, or other flexible or ductile materials. A mesh is similar to a web or a net in that it has many attached or woven strands.

AI MESH

2

GOVERNMENT NOTES

God has really blessed me as a White House Correspondent with WATB.tv to have access to government meetings, press conferences, press information, conferences, congresses, etc. He has provided us an inside look into this end-time scenario. In this chapter we will be privy to top-level government notes from the Vaccine Congress in 2020, DAVOS Meetings, UN Notes, etc.

In Fall of 2020, WATB Ministries hosted a Vaccine Congress. We participated in the Congress from Washington DC. We invited the Bride to come in and watch the presentations by the world leaders involved with this agenda of the COVID-19. These are the first time these notes will be seen. Now you will see what they said from the very beginning…

VACCINE CONGRESS NOTES

Q - How to implement to general population mass vaccination?
- Scenarios - High versus low-income challenges
  Workplace verses Pharmacy

- Challenges - Young mobile age groups
  - Trust
    - Establish is critical step
    - Obstacles in communication is key
    - Public listens is the goal
    - Tools - powerful is surveys
    - Topics covered by public
    - Sophisticated way is comp base/need funds

Create infrastructure for mass vaccinations

Groups -
- Elderly
- Adolescent
- childhood

Investments - train up and decisions made
Concerns
Criteria - introduce vaccine and funds

Mandatory Policies
- Send messages *This is important
- Serve purpose by creating checkpoints to measure yes or no of choice
- Healthcare workers must comply
- Nudge them through **peer pressure**
- **Create checkpoints**
- Basically, serve, create and nudge
- Make welfare conditional
- No jab no pay (Australia roll-out)
- People dependent on welfare/subsidizing influences choice to vax

Extremists are the ones who reference the vaccine & how to transmit disease
- Don't trust the vaccine
  - People don't trust vaccine because they think they're harmful, thus mandatory policies are helpful

- People don't trust more draconian approaches
  - Rigorous, unusually severe or cruel
  - Harsh marshal law
  - Punitive and severe
- Interventions to change behavior

FINANCIAL FACTORS INFLUENCES CORE
- Study of improving vaccination rates to the massive
  - Why it is so effective of getting on subsidies
  - People are dependent on government

To Mandate:
- Start out voluntary
  - Issue finances
  - Gain public support
- Implement no jab no pay
- No tax breaks
- Health insurance surcharge and vax rates
- Brings up equity issues/sliding scale
- Everybody WILL be vaccinated!

Hindrance Factors:
- People are too busy and out working
- Challenges based on low-income countries
- Ideologies is a hindrance factor!
- Vaccine hesitancy is anti-science!
- Trust in vaccines is linked to higher education and income

Combination Strategies:
- Inroad to mandatory vaccinations
  - Education
  - Workers
  - All done ToGetHer

- Give a sense of urgency with info to public
    - Reassure to take care of any issue
    - Line up for clinical trials once approved
- Demand generation at educational level
    - to trust system
    - Of vax process development
- Proliferate with fake news and make issues
    - Global impact with people taking vax

Image of the Vaccine
- Immunization to be seen as democratic intervention
- Invest responsibility of population to protect others
- Perception of other people
- You need to be vaxxed to protect others
- Right relationships with others include vaccination success
- Concept of herd immunity

Other Notes:
- Add new vax along with old
- Exponentially increase effectiveness w/emphasis on importance to coverage extremely high
- Differences between continents and similarities
- All states to require vax for school entry and police power
- US Constitution interpreted that states have the authority to require
- Defined variables in religious exemptions
- Discussed concerns for clustering of refusal to vax
    - Balance between personal autonomy and public health
        - Move towards protector of public health and reduce personal autonomy
            - Thus, restrict social gatherings
            - "I don't want to wear" mentality
        - Eliminate expense of autonomy

- Antibody is for previous exposure
    - PCR test is for current infection
    - T-Cell Testing
- Universal system is free
- Ideology is a social problem
- Are anti-vaxxers neo-Nazis?

Australian Experience of Mandatory Policy:
- Removed non-medical exemption
- More trust and accepting governing authority
- Parents will not receive subsidy if baby is not vaccinated

Financial incentives to vax
- No jab no pay brought vax rates up to 94%
- Daycare payments are powerful incentives to target age groups
- Is this a good strategy?

Adverse Event:
- Get undermine public trust
- Equity considerations
    - Wealth
    - Ignore mandate
    - Subsidies
    - Poor can't afford not to
    - Informed consent

Italy -
- Fines are issued for those who are not vaccinated
- Optional versus non-optional
- Moved to mandatory because 85% not
- Backfire to mandatory

- o Coverage increased rapidly
- o Real polarization of society

Equity - main point is to offer intervention for everyone globally

Link -
- info/thoughts people who are vaccinated
- Attitude first
- With unvaxxed monitor trust
  - o Plan info campaign

Merch, Pfizer, Takeda & GSK Notes

Med-tech Sector -
- IMI Project
  - o Controlled human partnership

B&D Europe
- Geo-political to share information said before next virus pops up
- Therapeutics will help with new strains
- **Fast response to vaccines through blockchain to traceability**
  - o This is new technology
- **mRNA will it work for all targets?**
  - o It depends on the immune response
  - o Does each person need t-cells? It's not determined at this time.
  - o Immune system to cooperate with them

In Session 2
- Four years of Ebola vaccine really stressed the unity of the stakeholders

Jessica from HHS - Operation Warp Speed
- Colonel says "cost is no longer an element to consider"
- Surveillance is the heart of this
- Surveillance is the foundation of America

One Health Approach
- CDC organizes workgroup
    - Sustainability
    - G7
    - G20
    - Key piece of paradigm

Response to Vaccine
- People may be politically and socially exhausted
- Getting people in quarantine faster
- New Normal is:
    - 6-foot distancing
    - Hand washing
    - Masks
- #whyweexist

Nanoparticles
- #everyjourneymatters
- Novel technologies to monitor product quality in vaccine supply chains

RANDOM NOTE: Woods are now being monitored! Elon Musk sent out chips everywhere.

Science is a Social Justice!
America is the Leader of this Global Mission
- COVAX Facility @ GAVI Partners

- o Partner together for robust vaccine manufacturing & distribution

Rockefeller Founded GAVI
- Bill Gates gave 750 million for five years
- 750 million to GAVI

Rockefeller & Bill Gates is the glue that holds all these programs together.

World Economic Forum's Global Governance Summit Notes
Shaping the Future of Artificial Intelligence

Kay - Head of Ai & Machine Learning WEF
16 other projects under Ai to Leap frogging using Ai

Irene - The Straits Times - Hostess from Singapore

Impact on COVID using AI going Forward

Good morning, thank you, Kay. Good morning and welcome to our panel on shaping the future of artificial intelligence, **Irene, Straits Times**, a national daily newspaper in Singapore. And I'm your moderator today. And we hope to have a conversation on the impact and the effect of the COVID pandemic on AI and its governance and how AI can be used going forward. We saw AI's news accelerate as nations try flattening the COVID-19 infection curve even before AI rules and norms weren't yet in place. Many of these users required citizen to see forego their civil liberties and data protection rights. From robots that detect population movements and social gatherings in China, to aggressive tracing of the close contacts of the COVID patients using mobile location data in Israel and also credit card payments and facial data in South Korea, AI's use was nothing short of intrusive. When privacy is curtailed, it is important to revisit some of the government's gaffs and attempt to block them.

Failing to do so will have a long-term impact on public health and privacy policies. Also, the social contracts between our Governments and the citizens in industries involving the use of predictive algorithms may also need to be redrawn, hopefully after some robust discussions on AI ethics to maintain public trust in AI's use over the long-term. In fact, some say that these conversations are overdue, so at this juncture, I would like to introduce our distinguished panel to talk about how AI can be used responsibly and how everyone can shape the future to ensure that AI technology benefits everyone.

I would like to introduce Vilas, Patrick J. McGovern Foundation, a tech change-maker to use AI solutions to create an equitable future for all. Second, we have Mark, of Appen, a publicly traded company in Australia, and human annotated data set expert for training machines for machine-learning algorithms, and specifically Appen used tech and audio to improve AI systems. They know we have Haniyeh, at DataRobot, a Massachusetts-based company, implementing data usage for retail to healthcare, from antimony laundering, reducing false positives to laundry laundering, and reducing patient readmission rates.

And lastly, Jason, who works in the White House with a focus on Technology and National Security. He is the Deputy Assistant to the President for Technology and National Security, a new role he has taken on. Each speaker will have a chance to provide their perspectives on the topic, during which the audience can submit questions using the chat function. We will have a Q&A session later on to address as many of these questions as possible, so do ensure that your questions are concise and relevant to the topic. So now we will invite Vilas to offer a perspective on philanthropy to -how important is it for governments to have an AI policy and how can philanthropy put us on the road to supporting all of society.

Vilas - Patrick J. McGovern Foundation

Irene, the World Economic Forum has taken great leadership on these questions, and I'm the President of a civil society organization, The Patrick J. McGovern Foundation. And two observations:

1. I've spent most of my life as a technologist and a human rights advocate. And I have to share just how optimistic I am about the power of technology to make the human experience better. We're seeing it by the day in increasing agricultural yields and increasing access to education, finding new ways to express ourselves and form new connections.

2. But in the context of that very positive observation, I have to make the second, which is I feel like we're very quickly tagging onto a Navy, of a three-sided stool, where technology companies innovate, governments regulate, and third, where *We the People* become consumers rather than becoming cocreators.

Now, coming into civil society and to your question, Irene, it's not so much that any one of those single characterizations are wrong -- but I would say they are -- but what's broken down is a social compact, one that doesn't put technology in the center, but rather one that puts individual and collective interests at the center of the model. I think if we can get to the place where governments move first to understand their citizen's needs and trying to increase innovation in tools that lead to a better future, where technology companies treat participants as part of the design of the technology and see where individuals have a voice through civil society, that can lead to a fundamental new social compact for the AI age.

So, I'm excited for the large of the global AI action alliance, one of the core tenets of this program is to bring actors together in one inclusive environment where the question can go from "how do we build responsible and ethical AI?", to "what does an ethical society look like?" Jason, who works in the White House with a focus on Technology and National Security. AI allows for entirely new form of economic and social values. I'm excited to explorer those topics with you.

The pandemic has highlighted the opportunity to take that model that I'm describing and apply it at scale.

Irene: Thank you. Consumers should be treated as a stakeholder in the development of AI, rather than the outcome. So that's a good thought. So, let's hear from the private sector. Mark, as an executive of a layered in a company that is involved, what is your goal for AI, and what steps can companies do to get things right from the start? And if data is the starting point for training machines what, are the important considerations to data sets?

Mark: Thank you, Irene, and thank you everybody. It's a pleasure to be here. It's a pleasure to be part of the conversation at the forum. Data is a really important consideration, and there's a few things that we look at to make sure that we're sourcing AI and providing data responsibly. So, in short, the data becomes the AI. So, if you have, for example, a biased data set, you're going to get a biased AI outcome.

There are three areas that we look at when we look at data, and this builds on Vilas' comments about the role of cure. The first is data privacy. We -- the role of the consumer -- we make sure that we're consistent with all of the legislations around data privacy. That we seek consent at that time that we collect from people, etc. and so it's important, that we maintain those data that we collect, we maintain the security and the privacy of those throughout the use of that data.

The second area is data bias. Which is a topic that many people are familiar with in AI, quite simply, if you're trying to build a speech recognition product that works for all people, you need to collect data that is representative of all people, for example, representative tones of voice, representative accents. For example, if you have a data set exclusively of male voice, it's not going to work. The resulting AI is not going to work as well for female voices. So, it's important to have an unbiased data set. The other area, which is an area that gets some press, but perhaps not as much, is around the ethical sourcing of data, and this is not just a privacy issue, but the treatment of the people that prepare the attachment. We rely on a global crowd of over a million people to collect and label the data, and we have developed over time our own crowd of ethics that making sure that we're paying people correctly, being inclusive, that we're communicating our will to the crowd, etc.

And now, there are some legislations in this area, as we know, there's things like GDPR for data privacy, ISO standards 27,001 for security and protection of data, there are modern slavery legislations that ensure that people in every part of the value chain are treated fairly. But there are also some challenges, to Vilas' point about the role of the consumer. There's a certain tension in that.

First of all, data privacy legislation -- it varies by jurisdiction. Jurisdictions with lax data privacy that allow random data harvesting, ironically are going to build better AI because they have that, so there's that tension in privacy and the AI outcome.

The other area is that is also a challenge is in the area of data bias. So, to go back to the previous example, on voice tone, in order to round down a data set, for example, if you have a lot of male voice tones, you have to discriminate in your data collection and collect female voice tones only, and that becomes a bit of a challenge when we're trying to do everything fairly and openly.

So, the completeness and the fairness of the data sets are important contributor to AI. We do a number of things at Appen that support supports those things, but there's work to go done in this area because it's very inconsistent across the globe and across jurisdictions.

Irene: Thank you, Mark. Now, we turn to Jason for government voice. You serve as commissioner on the Pentagon National House Security Commissions on Artificial Intelligence, and the commissions recommended last month several changes to the national AI policy that you now oversee at the White House.

So, from your perspective, how can AI be used responsibly? Perhaps with specific measures where possible, and also addressing the questions we ask, how important is it for governments to have a strong AI and data science policy or strategy?

Jason: Thanks, Irene. It's about pleasure to be here with so many friends, who I know are in the audience and on this panel. And just as the history of AI is one of international collaboration, so will be its future.

So, there's two parts of AI where I think government need to be especially mindful, and where the international community needs to be especially active. And that's first advancing privacy preserving AI, and second, advancing safe AI.

On privacy, our global approach needs a revamp. In a recent survey of American attitudes towards AI, respondents' number one concern was that AI-assisted surveillance would violate privacy and civil liberties. Europe has one of the most comprehensive regulations in the world, but it has more or less the same technical vulnerability to say privacy as existed before. There is privacy-preserving AI such that can achieve both our privacy goals as well as the performance goals. And further off we have the prospect of fully homomorphic encryption, so that we can protect data while at rest, in motion, and during processing.

So, one goal for us both in the United States, but also, I think internationally, is to ensure that our national and international standards for AI, such as those that are being developed under ISOS342 are compatible with privacy-protecting methods. And I think we should work collaboratively in the international research community to refine those privacy-preserving methods, so that we can achieve our privacy goals and performance goals simultaneously. Safety is another area both for national attention and for international collaboration. We don't yet have design principles to provide safety guarantees in AI.

The United States supports both the OECD AI principles, and the work ever the global partnership on AI, both of which emphasize the robust and secure systems, and that are safe, but we need ways to reliably measure those processors. We don't have those methods currently.

We also need to work towards technical standards, and measurement approaches to make safe AI systems.

I think one opportunity for international collaboration is a shared tech bed in which to test methods against known failure modes and to develop new methods for measuring robustness under a variety of conditions. So, I look forward to the discussion of these, and finding ways to cooperate so that we achieve progress on both.

Irene: Thanks, Jason. On the point you mentioned about international cooperation, this is a point which I'll ask Haniyeh as well later on. Social norms vary from place to place. **CCTV and robot surveillance may be accepted in one place and rejected in another, and there is no one-size-fits-all solution.**

How do you ensure that this cooperation achieve the objectives that will be beneficial to all the stakeholders as part of these cooperation he was the? Jason, perhaps you could take the question first, and then later I'll turn to Haniyeh to talk about some of the more overarching universal principles that may apply and work.

Jason: Yeah. I mean, I think that we have birthed a variety of principles that almost every AI developer in almost every country on the planet are going to agree are important, or that we should aspire to have our AI systems' robustness, ensuring that a system operates within safe limit -- assurance so, to establish that it can be analyzed and understood easily by human operators.

Specification, ensuring that it's align winning the system designer's intentions. Those are all properties that not only developers aspire to, but also that citizen and see policymakers aspire to. So, I think there's actually enormous room for agreement on many of these principles.

Irene: Okay, cool. Haniyeh, would you like to provide your perspective from how some companies have operationalized some of these universal ethical principles in their implications.

Haniyeh: Global Ai Ethicist

Sure, absolutely. Yeah, it's kind of like following up on what Jason was saying, there are some processes that everyone can agree on. The way to collect the data. There should be consent around it. You know, as Mark was talking about, about the bias that can appear in the dark. How can we address that? And -- in the data -- and putting in protections in place for the users to be able to understand and recognize the problem, so they would be able to take action based on that. And also, kind of understanding, as you mentioned, these norms can be different. What we define as a protected class in the US may not apply to other countries. So, it's not understanding what's the main goal and objectives for us.

Whether it's about fairness for example. What is it that we are trying to achieve? I think we can have a common ground in that area and work on the details for each region separately.

Irene: Right. On some of the technical metrics mentioned earlier -- Jason touched on federated learning, and ensuring that data at rest and data in process is encrypted. There are also a couple of other measures, like being transparent about what data is used to train algorithms, and revealing if algorithms can generate consistent results across a diverse range of people, and the margin of error, you know, and revealing what the margin of error is, it will go a long way to build trust in AI, but AI practitioners, are they to that go today? Is it lacking?

Vilas Dhar - Patrick J. McGovern Foundation

Are there areas which we can improve on? Anybody can take this question.

Vilas: I'll jump in. I like the question -- I think you're right that AI practitioners are beginning to have these conversations about how we apply the technical elements to go back to the sourcing of detachment, but I might just suggest we take one step further back. You asked a question about how regional and national differences perceive acceptable norms should define our ways we deploy AI. And I would suggest there is a moment to reconceptualize exactly what the interests of the individual are, in a data-driven economy.

We talk about privacy and making sure that the data is representative, but we never go down to asking what are an individual's real interests in their data? And how do we conceptualize the AI process that recognizes that individuals might have more rights in data that they use, not just in privacy, but being able to control on how the data is used and being able to vote on how the data is used by AI practitioners.

We need a conversation that starts with the interests and vulnerabilities of the model and then translates into how we build a responsible AI framework that integrates those interests. That conversation allows us to step out of the national frameworks that we're currently using, and even as we think about international cooperation to start again from a core conception of where the individual sits in the framework.

Fayaz - Deputy Exec Director Field Results & Innovation UNICEF

Thank you, Irene, and thank you very much to our wonderful panelists tonight. It's now my great pleasure to introduce Mr. Fayaz and invite him to give closing remarks for today's session. Mr. King is Deputy Executive Director, field results and innovation at UNICEF. He is also a member of the forum's global AI Council and has vociferously for more international cooperation for the development and deployment of responsible AI, especially as it relates to those who will be impacted most by the policies that we develop today -- the world's youth.

Fayaz: Thank you, Kay. I think we've heard this evening the words accountability, transparency, and impartiality. These are fundamental elements of any ethical and human rights-based endeavor, especially in the field of AI.

This has made today's discussion very, very fruitful. I'd like to put a child lens on all of this. If AI works for children, it works for everyone. So, by applying the child lens to everything we do, we take care of generation AI. It's today's children: those who use or are impacted by AI for their healthcare, their schooling, their communication, and eventually the jobs that they'll do.

So, anything we do with respect to AI, we need to consider the children. When AI works for children, it works for everyone. At UNICEF, we have a policy for the guidance of AI for children, which we've developed in partnership with the government (word) and it's encouraging to see that other governments are picking up on this and adopting this and putting this into their national policies. In May this year, we will be releasing the good governance for children's data manifesto, so please stay tuned for this.

But what's also important to note is that the AI gap is exponential, as compared to the digital divide. We've heard the term digital public goods, and at UNICEF, we are cohosts of the digital public goods alliance in collaboration with Norway to make data, content, all open sources. We also heard the term of generation equality and in technology and innovation, of how governments and private sectors can work together and put all the pieces together to form policies that help with children and everything that they do. This is a once-in-a-generation opportunity to positively impact children's lives everywhere. I consider it a privilege today to listen to the various perspectives being put forward, and for the various questions that were raised on the floor. In closing, I think it's important that we all collaborate, we work together with government, we work together with entrepreneurs, both those established and aspiring. I think we can work together to shape a brighter future for AI. And if I can close by saying, if AI works for children, it will work for everyone. Thank you, Kay.

Kay: Thank you very much, Fayaz. And what a wonderful and inspiring thing to say: If it works for children, it works for everyone. And yet, you're absolutely right, that we need to be mindful of the people for whom we are thinking about, to we regulate, don't we regulate. What do companies do? What don't companies do? And so, thank you so much for those very inspiring remarks. It's been an absolute pleasure as well for us to be able to work with you, and Henrietta at UNICEF, and many of your colleagues generally on shaping the technology to envisage excellent outcomes. And we have the smart toys initiative for which she will be a judge. We've also been working on UNICEF to creating an AI youth council, because as Vilas so wonderfully put it, we need to really extend the number of people who are past our discussions on AI, and that should include young people from all over the world. And so, we're really looking for one person, one child, from each country, to about 30 in that council. And that's just one of the very many things that we do on the AI platform at the World Economic Forum.

DAVOS 2022 TECHNOLOGY COOPERATION SPONSORED BY WORLD ECONOMIC FORUM JANUARY 2022

Technology Coop.in the 4th Ind. Revolution

-Digital

If you are not connected, you cannot use the important services

Services:
- Mobility
- Cloud

-To connect people (ALL status) to bring them healthcare etc.

-Human rights to BE Connected

-Bring them the technology

Strong Digital Infrastructure

-Proceed w/ green transitions of technology to better systems of COVID

-Doing this TOGETHER

-Sustainable systems

-Recovering from the "depth" of financial fractures

*Failing vaccinating ALL means that more variants will emerge - *Antonio Guterres - UN*

Antonio Guterres/UN

-To fix it, ALL humanity needs to jump on board!

-"Preparing for the next PANDEMIC with Universal Health Care"

-Bringing a new Financial System

-...emerging economies!

-Climate change is affecting the economy

-Goal: emissions reductions

-Emerging Economies...

To accelerate the transition

Technical support

- With partnerships (alliance)
- Economical support

NET ZERO Goal by 2050

-Need to speed up the "TRANSITION"

-United: "We need to come TOGETHER"

-Climate change Goal:

-Decarbonizing the Globe

Social Fractures Fixing Goals:

-Renewed "Social Contract"

-"Private Sector" is key

    -Support from the outside
    -"New Global Deal"
    -Private investments
    -International Financial Inst. partnering with private sector
    DAVOS 2022 - Meeting the Challenge of Vaccine Equity

Michael- WHO Health Emergencies Program

Over half the world - ½ the population have received two doses of the vaccine (Africa -only 7%)

- Vaccines are central strategic pillar in ending pandemic phase-no other way out

    Distributing vaccines equitably is required to end pandemic

Most scarce commodity in this pandemic is TRUST (between government and communities, between manufacturers and purchasers, between countries) multilayer

We are faced with an existential crisis as a race and as a civilization on this planet - current mechanisms in place for production of vax do not lead to the equitable distribution.

    -we have a virus that's killing millions of people, disrupting our hospitals, our society's

    -everybody is responsible/in charge because everybody is at risk

-create technology at transfer hubs

- look at every aspect of the system / multi layered approach / targeted change

Other challenges ahead

- current global multisystem NOT fit for purpose for dealing with the threat

- production of vax (if current production is adequate currently why aren't the vax with the people who need it?)

-distribution / production needs to be more strategically planned down to the last mile

Private and public sector engagement required to participate in solutions

We have a responsibility to come out of this pandemic with answers to assist in handling the next pandemic.

COVAX primary aim - vaccinate 10% most vulnerable then became 20%- healthcare workers and elderly - worldwide all at the same time. This didn't happen.

-believes this is still very important and possible

Focus on the future - may need 3-4 doses right away for proper coverage

We may never end the virus this year, it may never end, it will become a part of the ecosystem - we can end the public health emergency that was instated Jan 2020

Death, hospitalizations, disruption of social economic political systems cause of tragedy - the virus is the vehicle – it's how society has reacted that is the tragedy

Endemic just means the virus is here forever

Seth - Gavi, the Vaccine Alliance
We are not behind; The target of 950 million doses to AMC countries by end of 2021 was met

Monday April 5, 2021
Global Technology Governance Summit
Japan organized event
leaders across all disciplines and technologies
non-fungible NFT's

Sheila - Centre for 4th Ind. Rev. Network (4IR)
-Government Services
    private/public media academia
-creation, deployment, and use of tech
-make sure we don't exploit vulnerable population
-a chance to reinvent healthcare

Mark - Salesforce

Inflection of Davos 2020 and accelerated at Davos this year

Climate change his #1 priority

1T.org - Plant 1 trillion tree initiative to sequester 200 trillion gigatons carbon

Salesforce with WEF - creating the 5 Industrial Revolution

Ecopreneurs - 10,000 have come into uplink how do we accelerate our march towards reducing climate change. Netzero - Japan how we emit less

-how do we sequester carbon? Renovation of Green, blue, brown, and grey carbons

low hanging satelites to quantify carbon

use biometricians tech to improve multi stakeholder dialog accelerating path to Netzero

C02 is #1 issue on planet today on how to change of shape climate change

ESG

We can be carbonized, use technology to improve the state of the world

Vivian

Minister of Foreign affairs Singapore

-Greener, fairer, smarter world (1. Do people trust technology, 2. Utility)

-Covid helped to turbocharge (Covid has been a stress test)

-Contact tracing

    Bluetooth proximity tracing

    4-day to 1 1/2-day process

    Always silver lining

    catalyst, stress test capability

    resilient, sustainable

95% transactions in Singapore are cashless

Need more resilience and greener world

Susan - YouTube

-accelerated online education learning job creation

-huge innovation in medical early detection

-ability to learn almost anything get trained for a skill

-further grow human capital

-tell stories that would not have been told

-underrepresented groups

-large diversity of content

-payment majority of revenue to creators over $30 B in 3 years

-medical - she is excited

- drug development, early detection, AI, enable people to live longer, healthier lives
- YouTube-Global Video Library –
- access to information. Over 75% people used YouTube this year during pandemic

Crypto & Bitcoin – Why Christians Must Not Participate

Hiroaki - Hitachi
- Technology 5.0
- Why Governance matters is the work of WEF
- Companies being fully transparent / equal pay
- tech for military use
- how to use tech to solve social issues
- his background computer/system design
- very optimistic for future tech.
- YouTube says - they work with governments around the world.

Challenges;
- -speech, -what should/should not be allowed,
- -legal but harmful content. AI is compliant, anything that government says is illegal they won't have on at all.
- effectiveness of global tracking- battle of extremism (different understanding what privacy is)

Take better care of the oceans - dolphins and whales
- USB & WEF - by drone technology can tell a ship of a whole hit before it happens

Sheila - we have to work together

VB - Do people believe tech is for their good?
1.) question about trust needs to be addressed
2.) Does the tech work?
   Covid has been the stress test for this

MB- Society 5.0

SW- we work closely w/governments around the world lots of challenges

    1.) Speech- what should/not be allowed?
- content may be legal that might be seen as harmful . e.g., COVID-19
- effective - different organizations when they come together
- violent extremism
- climate change, unbanked
- how do create global consensus

HN-

    1.) trust

    2.) how to utilize data to see what is happening

    3.) to build up the trust

        starting points

        secure + safer

        build up trust building approach

MB- stop killing whales/dolphins

        through strikes

        tech. developed by UCSB   wellsafe.com

Ocean - AI combined w/ audio and drones
- Ecopreneurs like Doug McCauly
- created whale.com which is why he's excited about tech

SW- vaccines

don't want silos, move world toward more cooperative model

VB- digital world is merging with real world in real world you wouldn't accept that everything goes
- hate speech or divisive speech
- does internet myths need a reboot
- I don't think in real world we have adapted to the scalability of internet
- speed of light

SW- agrees that NOT everything goes
- YouTube has put in tremendous policies - tech enabled because of AI

Policies –
- identify videos out of compliance, anything a government bans they don't put on YouTube.
- Legal but potentially harmful is the grey area.
- Sometimes there are a lot of differences between governments.
- The more digging the more complicated.
- Make best decisions together to keep communities safe.

MB- Singapore greatest challenges becoming Netzero
- 50 million tons CO2 per year. How do they create a bank to reduce those tons?
- Biodiversity to preserve and conserve.

VB- 1/3 Singapore covered with trees and more biodiversity than the entire US

    Greener, fairer and smarter

SW- how do we think across our silos w/ either industry, etc.

    GIFCT

    Global Internet Forum For Counter Terrorism

Shaping the future of the Data Economy

By the age of 18, person is defined by at least 70,000 data points

Sheila - Head of Blockchain and Data Policy - Member of Executive Committee of WEF
- poses solutions we need to shape together
- how we form tech tomorrow depends on decisions we make today.

Kabir – Moderator - OneTrust
- managing the trust and personalization
- People's interests and best practices

JoAnn - MasterCard
- people own their own data
- people centered design
- about individuals, making their lives safe, simple and smart
- how do we design
- transparent about data practices- AI
- encourage privacy and security

- navigate data ecosystems
- social innovation

Juan - Secretary of Digital Innovation -- City of Medellin, Columbia
- Lack of trust in government
- stakeholders - trust in our citizens to give their data
- open dialogue, collective way
- starting point for creating
- auditing policies for stakeholders
- support in opportune way based on data

Jennifer - The Commons Project
- 80% inequality
- regulators focused on top-down
- bottom up is important to empower individual
- putting data ownership and privacy up front - not a lot of options in owning data
- Data is valuable and powerful
- Trust is really currency

Maria - UN office of the Envoy on Technology
- Equitable/inclusive way to include those who can't afford access
- data economy
- innovation, social objective
- multi-stakeholder approach (framework for our action)

- social and sustainability goals, human rights aspects, right of privacy and security
- fundamental right/not privilege
- roadmap for digital cooperation - Document UN
- Grassroots
- Focusing on sustainable development
- Role of technology in protecting humanity

KB-
- People-first innovation- more equal development
- How can better manage relations between people and tech
- Responsible tech practices

JS-
- equitable
- build intelligent society deliberate and party's
- AI to prevent teenage pregnancy between 10 - 21 (and child development)
- Guarantee high speed internet at low prices
- integrate system for monitoring food, so that reach kids w/ malnutrition, physical and mental health
- ethical use of info
- 3.7 million - 450,000 educational institutions and platforms combine data
- Police cert.
- workers - homes check physical and mental health
- check family violence

- Malnutrition, economic divide
- access to high-speed internet
- AI predicting pregnancy, physical health, mental health

MFS- trust comes w/more general trust in government

JSG- providing connectivity to all

JZS- once you're trusted, always trusted
- trust is earned
- global infrastructure
- owned by individuals regardless of nationality
- think about what kind of infrastructure should be global

JS- entering what comes out of COVID
- Pandemic - vaccines - vaccine passports - AI - info shared
- Trust but also harm
- Wild ride around a case of tech
- Needed changes happening public - individual private roles
- Need more commonality, common platforms
- Payment's ecosystems have responsible players inclusive
- If you don't have info about all of society - inequities
- Improve data quality, info sharing without sharing personal, choice
- Rights vs. liabilities
- COVID forcing function- data across borders
- Info sharing

MFS- how data is utilized, stored, shared
- core set of principles missing per UN
- equal protection for all individual

JZS-
- laws allow citizens to have input on data and its use
  - use data understand citizens to meet their needs
  - security safety health employment
  - empower them w/ software and hardware
  - education and prevent malnutrition

JS- innovate next generation services + products

SW-
- inflection point due to pandemic
  - empowering individuals
  - creating policies addressing inequities
  - people-centered design
  - people-first economy
  - circular economy
  - social credit system

The Next Frontier Synthetic Biology

Geny (GD) Head Transformation at WEF
  - Frontier where **biology and tech are mixing**

Mariette (MD) College of Communication
   MODERNA - Modify DNA - electronic

Megan (MP) Bio Policy and Leadership Initiatives / Stanford University
  - Synthetic Bio. - community, field & approach
  - engr., bio, art, design, humanities

- make bio easier to engineer
- programming functions in DNA/ evolution; Crispr is helping
- over 40 years ago - first designed recombinant DNA
- Approach synthesis is important to the way to learn engineer a world in which we want to live
- Billions of years of evolution behind it already - evolution becomes a tool

Jason (JK) Gingko Bioworks
- Impossible Burger
- Found DNA code to make code for hemoglobin brewed it in w/ yeast, programming that yeast
- mRNA vax is installing mRNA in your body- **piece of RNA code**, says temporary spike protein from virus primes immune system

Margaret (MH) Global Bio Policy & Programs NJI
- Medicine, Manufacturing, food
- Risks- responsible conduct new areas of science and create framework for responsible stewardship
- Bio terrorism, more transmissible virulent able to elude vaccines
- Misused: deliberate use of inadvertent release of synthetic Bioweapon- create new organisms
- For example - more robust harvest, resistant crops may have negative impacts elsewhere

- equity and fairness avail to all (not only the wealthy countries) or only those with considerable resources
- Inadvertent release of a product that could cause harm - drought resistant robust harvest

Matthew (MC) National University of Singapore
- balance opportunities and risks for synthetic bio
- mean diff. things to diff. countries, cultures, etc.
- long history of engagement w/ stakeholders
    - need broader base of stakeholders, greater accountability and trust
    - collaborative and adaptable
- risks also mitigated by scientific innovation
- good global oversight recognized by public will increase knowledge of risks and public trust
- focus on the "future we want" across the globe
- learn from past what worked, what didn't
- stay ambitious and humble

MC-
- synth bio- viewed as tech that can widen inequalities and environmental destruction
- anxiety across globe, share benefits across globe - establish consensus
- viewed as difficult & costly, very futuristic and resource intensive

- how can be more affordable without international cooperation, synth bio will lift only a few boats, not the rising tide

MH-FDA / Global Governance
- life span approach
- multi-faceted approach
- think about projects conceptualization - research at university (oversight needed at all levels) - industry oversight at institutional
- currently not focus at global level
- normative entity engaging with all stakeholders for global governance needed
- oversight includes national regulation and global needs
- need global common standards

MP- Values to think about
- global future council co-chairing with Aust.
- diff regions of world, developing ways to engage everyone
- "realize potential for global common good"
- protect our health
- solutions to processing global challenges
- climate change
- next generation vaccines, not being made everywhere
- what are ethical strategies to get there
- values: bio securing equity, sustainability, solidarity, humility, need to be careful. Interface could be us.

- biowarfare and synthetic bio to protect our health
- next gen vaccines - global future council - ethical strategies
- equity(prioritize), humility, solidarity, how do we support each other across the scales
- sustainability how to coexist with biosphere
- a lot to learn about bio, need to be careful and focus on problems that bio can solve
- a lot of her work on biosecurity - deliver efficiently and well
- innovation & governance
- developing ways to engage many global communities
- tech transfer
- equity needs to be financial

JK- Values from industry- horizontal platform (e.g., YouTube)
- Gingko horizontal platform program a cell - self-fertilizing corn?
- Can't have attitude that it's just a tool don't care how it is used
- **bio is programmable - DNA**
- moves atoms around, things that matter more must care how the tools are used
- stewardship, multi stakeholder CONVO, real security is int'l bio doesn't respect borders, global biosecurity

JC- hope rising tide of synthetic bio will life all boats

MA- maybe see COVID put behind us and apply lessons we're all in it together, science knows no borders
- -getting vax into people's arms in less than a year
- -align power of science with medical

Enabling the Future of Mobility

Reduce emission

Public acceptance

Christopher (CW) Head of Shaping the Future of Mobility / WEF
- Israel is a startup nation - autonomous vehicles
- Limited resources,
- huge potential for private autonomous vehicles to reduce accidents

Ofer (OM) Ministry of Transportation and Road Safety of Israel
- Israel lacks natural resources so rely on tech innovation
- autonomous vehicles (will be public, not privately owned)
- key elements for the private sector to save savings.
- Will release people to save money to raise their lifecycle
    - limited # of railways
- huge incentive to move to autonomous vehicles
- less accidents and deaths by accidents w/auto vehicles

Shauna (SM) Sense Photonics, Inc.
- business model must be viable
- cost of these vehicles, must be ready for mass manufacturing

- vehicle miles down during pandemic and accidents on the rise

Tom (TP) Wingcopter GmbH
- Knowledge to train people to drive the drones, to deliver medicines and vaccines.
- highway in the sky - this is a billion-dollar industry.
- So many cases for drones.
- unmanned delivery drones
- trained people in Mulawi to use them
- partner with UNICEF
- transport medicines, highway in the sky
- acceptance, cost efficiency
- start with unmanned delivery drones
- establish locally
- policy that is adaptive / enabling infrastructure / innovations

Mekapati (MR) Commerce & Information Tech of Andhra Pradesh Policy by 2024
- 3 or 4 major cities will be going off engines
- policy needs to adaptive in the sense that it can catch up with technology
- going to bring in new pattern of mobilization
- creating first drone city
- Diagrams must be backed by plan of skilled workers
- -new scaling of skilled workers

- **OM-** How far out are you from deploying level 3
  - can private owners be trained to drive and maintain
  - Readiness in cities-based context
    - They are testing in Jerusalem now. He drove there in autonomous vehicle in TelAviv 100's of robot taxis
  - Private owned or companies
  - In larger perspective - batteries cost a lot. The more you sell, cost will drop, but he doesn't think so
  - Lithium battery limited supply, cost won't decrease
  - private owner sale won't work - 2nd hand market
  - battery cost as much as new car
  - a city where only AV exist - smart city good test, traffic control, safety, sensors, security
  - facing a lot of philosophical ethical questions
  - Tested 50 drones in orbital environment for delivering (medicine and other)
  - 100's missions per day
  - How to control it
  - Startups, etc. Israel seen as startup nation
    - -scaling them up need public acceptance
- **SM-** how to gain public trust
  - What do we deploy?
  - How reliable is that tech?
  - Trucks that do 1 M miles/year
  - Redundancy, sensors to detect obstructions in road

- The "what" needs to be safe
- The "how" to deploy safe and scalable transporting goods before people
- The environment? if you can control it incrementally expand presence of autonomous vehicles carefully

TP- drones in populated environments seen as not safe yet.
- Current climate? pioneering, early stages.
- How many drones around world?
- less population due to other energy sources
- work w/ FAA and other regulatory bodies
- testing and bold approaches
- Flying in 5 continents now, crop monitoring
- Next generation safety
- Setting up smart city for drones to fly
- right now, starting in rural areas
- Bold approaches and partnerships
- wants cross - border flights soon
- lots of people still needed to man the drones until AI takes over
- lots of money will be spent and lost on failures

SM- You learn more from failures than you do successes

MR- When we solve a problem, don't create another one
- Keep creating momentum
- Subsidize innovations, work step in step with industry
- we have a huge demand

- o data utilization in Mumbai greatest in the world
- o reduction of pesticides cuts down on carbon emissions
- o industry and government should be walking hand in hand

OM- Should be pushed by government regulation in order to improve lifestyle and safety

SM- Revamped coast to coast framework

TP- bold approaches, should not leave people behind

MR- Convergence, policy, regulation
- o Governments need to push this autonomous (to improve people's lifestyles), not corporations.
- o USA nor very acceptable, needs testing on safety in all areas. Be bold not scared.
- o "Convergence"

Technology Governance Outlook

All of the sessions have mentioned how the pandemic has helped or accelerated them to start and get everything going.

Jeremy (JJ) World Economic Forum

Elizabeth (ER) AZA Luxembourg
- o Considering startups as equals

Alice, Imperial College London
- o Public education is going to be very important

Sharon (SB) WEF
- o New social contract

- Jobs, rights, gender equality
- 40% world population doesn't have access
- monopolies, geopolitical
- Tech gov. how to put people in the middle
- Need Paris agreement or global treaty on technology governance

Jim (JHS) Siemens
- Best of times, worst of times
- Now at inflection point - can make energy systems
- preventive healthcare, technology already exists
- good business to solve problem
- Using tech in ways not very intelligent
- creating data monopolies, not equalizing
- may be solving wrong problems in wrong way
- COVID can be accelerator for digital future
- ability to implement at high speed (weeks vs months or years)
- What do we want tech to do?
- "We can have carbon neutral transportation"

ER- no large company can compete with small nimble
- election violence, flooding, fires, everything going wrong, partners new on scene, frontier markets (e.g., Nigeria)
- can partners produce needed error rates
- large companies went completely offline for months

- less transit time got more out of employees
- SB- 60% of world workers works informally
- at maximum, 30% remote working, isolation
- future is a hybrid one
- companies not transforming
- surveillance economy
- 2/3 of jobs are insecure
- technology must be integrated into work, but cannot ignore the down sides
- avoid stifling innovation
- find future tech is harnessed for good
- real commitment to shared property

JHS- don't mentally try to protect the jobs, but try to protect the people

- use true nature of human beings for creativity
- use robots to do repetitive jobs
- Pre-skilling the young and reskilling old is a big effort at Siemens so they become relevant, good for people and good business instead of laying off, now restructuring involves reskilling with tech developments.
- regulation vs innovation balance
- how to use data w/o losing privacy?
- Digital allows you to do things you could never do in the physical world.

- o Need more AI to do it morally

AG- reskilling and preskilling
- o education is so important to good governance, better progress on understanding to build trust

JJ- tech moving so fast, hard for the governments to keep pace
- o still balancing positives with challenges
- o human-centric technology
- o keeping people in dialog
- o Israel - Testing autonomous public transportation - Big experiment coming to Tel AVIV.
- o Using lithium, lithium is in shortage.

The Next Frontier: Space Technologies

Sarah- (SYA) Advanced Technology within the Ministry of Industry and Advanced Technology in the Government of the United Arab Emirates, chair of the UAE Space Agency and the United Arab Emirates
- o Impact arriving to Mars

George - (GW) Space Advisory Board / Virgin Galactic Advisory Board
- o Space can track fires, human trafficking

William Marshall (WM) - Co-founder and Chief Executive Officer / Planet Labs
- o satellite tech can help with at least 13 of 17 SDG's

- monitor nature
- 200 to monitor earth, landmass, waters - 25% of earth is land
- agriculture, improve crop yields by 20-40%
- protect deforestation of tropics
- need high resolution imagery, tree by tree
- sustainable fishing practices
- can detect illegal fishing activities
- they take their beacons off
- 10x10x30 cm weigh 5 kg - can play with it on your phone
- applications on earth - scan QR code and play (even cooler) w/ satellite
- Satellites help us see it all every day. Can tell when a farmer needs water or fertilizer for their crops (can evaluate not just photograph) and is able to single out almost every single tree.
- QR code for augmented reality. You can play with their spacecraft. 200 in orbit, taking pictures everyday of communication fleets.

Anousheh (AA) X Prize Foundation
- A lens not under the cloud.
- Democratize access to space
- constrained by cost of launch right now

Moore's Law – shrinking tech
- return examine our own Planet but Rest of universe
- Help us better understand our world is changing
- Weather pattern, how people changing, Manufacturing in space, ups for solar energy
- Cost to access space going down now

Francois (FG) Telecom Airbus
- Pandemic – not only a right to connect people but a necessity (can connect people anywhere)
- Outside cities, getting connection can be difficult, space can be that solution, in a year from now, can connect anyone anywhere in efficient way
- OneWeb - Airbus achievement
- Ships going into space.

WM – pollution in space environment
- 100 million pieces of space debris
- 30000 satellites on 3000 active - the remainder is space debris
- Keeping satellite slow enables self-destruction / self-cleaning
- Hire 800 to 1200 km need to clean up those lower orbits, space collision avoidance
- Blowing up satellites create big debris field

- Even if 1 in 1000 fails, that can be a big problem, keep them in LEO.

AA- need agreement on space, International treaty

SYA- overarching government does not impose inhibitions of spacecraft development
- New technologies to clean up space rather than having the orbiting capabilities on each spacecraft
- Change Norm of spacecraft design
- You don't need to own the spacecraft to benefit from it

AA – excited about new launch systems
- Also, further faster
- Laser-based launch system
- Elevator space-based

FG- commercial, navigation, weather, connect a craft, you can land it

WM– Revolution going on, dramatically increasing satellites right now
- Map of all world's coral reef
- Tracking tropical forest help indigenous people manage their Forest
- Using data to help us
- Over the next ten years, it will be an exciting ride because of all the data, AI.

GW- space governance thoughts?

WM- Wild West right now – make sure everyone can access it, without being too restrictive
- Example accessing water on the South Pole of the Moon, who owns it?

AA- climate Some Nations have Advantage currently
- All Nations requires collaboration
- come together, collaborate make things equitable

Nikolai- Space and Mobility/ WEF
- 6 ways space can benefit life on Earth
- Sustainability
- ESA
- Space governance
- Space junk management

Leading Industry Transformation

Jim - Member of BoT of the WEF
- 4 IR is about speed not size
- Next big infrastructure is digital
- We've got large problems let's use digital technology to solve them

Ana- Prime Minister of Serbia
- Digitization pays off 100% education empowers people to release creativity
- Forced into change

- o EU countries much stronger, they don't have driven to change they will pay for that later
- o E government
- o 7 million inhabitants of Serbia
- o Saved 180 million papers with electronic government
- o 900 tons of paper, 18000 trees, 76 million L of water, 6000 megawatts electricity
- o Multilateralism – Alliance of multiple countries pursuing a common goal
- o Need to go back to multilateralism, vaccines would have been different

The Honorable Koike- Government of Tokyo
- o Smart City Tokyo
- o Connected by IoT
- o Digital technology should be adjusted to people
- o 14 million inhabitants
- o 36 million surrounding area
- o Covid and climate change
- o App allows users to avoid heavy traffic on trains
- o No time to lose, now is the time to act
- o Harness power of digital transformation to achieve sustainable recovery

Dr. Youchi- Asia Pacific Initiative

Hanzade- Hepsburada

- Rebalance technology and individual companies that have had trouble pre pandemic won't survive
- Don't make pandemic a cover for what won't survive anyways

Scaling up Digital Identity Systems

Estimated 1 billion still lacking identification

CV- Omidyar Network
- SDG space 16.9 space legal ID for all

Mykhailo- Minister of Digital Transformation of Ukraine
- Launch fastest birth of new citizen
- Legalize digital ID, enable all life situation with
- Electronic digital signature embedded within smartphone
- Key in smartphone
- Within three years create
- Cybersecurity
- 10 million of 37 million use their app / digital service
- Fight corruption, monitor self-isolation covid pandemic accelerated progress, people demanding Digital Services
- No choice but to trust technology
- Decisions made faster. online, entire world moving faster in next 24 months
- Keep developing app to help people self-isolate, don't have to stand in lines, stay at home and don't contact who they don't want to contact

Don- Open Identity Foundation
- Value ownership and exchanges via IP
- Web 3.0 blockchain
- Cogs 4IR building blocks - UN blue
- Makes Ukraine inoperable, he has to complement Federov
- Unlocking value

Pandemic impact- accelerate to business problems
- fraud has increased in financial systems dramatically during this time
- more identity theft if we only get tech right, that is sound of one hand clapping, technology tools, government legislation and registration needed to scale identity systems

Smartphones converge several Technologies
- Facial recognition
- Geo-location
- Governance
- in user experience allows any kind of uses

Arrival of the Token Economy, from Art to Real Estate

2018 $310 million NFT

2020 $338 million NFT
- NFT= Non-fungible tokens
- NFT phenomenon - new token, world of tokens now
- Powerful intervention
- Building the blockchain - Center of the Beast

- Enables network computers to take collective data in database
- Decentralized economy
- COGS - IOT 4th industrial revolution.

Minister Abdulla (ABT) UAE
- Go double Economy in next decade
- 1.5 to 3 trillion Dirhams in the next decade
- Tokenization - fractionalization of assets, privately issued tokens, database of consumer
- Able to open economy for tokenization Behavior
- Sometimes we overregulate, lack of harmonized Regulation across jurisdiction
- Lack of adequate regulation
- Dubai future Association Center of 4 IR, Davos 2021 allow UAE to be a test bed for this technology
- Fractionalization of RE: use cases, brilliant monetization collectively level ownership, sustainability of renewable energy
- UAE invites other reasons to join them, scale digital assets

Harry: Reeps 100 studios, This & That art is the face of the token
- Carbon footprint of crypto, I'm collecting results in a chunk of Amazon rainforest.
- It is a concern
- Government should look at artist for answers
- Their job to engage, explore technology, bring questions to spaces, kick up noise to experts

- NFT artwork
- Ethereum BC
- Medium of permanence, brand new ways to collect
- Tokenization acceptance relies on demystification
- Everything you buy can now be tokenized common, Ledger of everything
- Smart contracts
- Provable scarcity valuable to artists use of immutability, digital becoming more real everyday

Sheila: - Head of Blockchain and Data Policy, WEF

Tip of the iceberg

ETFs example of portfolio of assets

- Generational Gap, and bedding voting rights into this ownership, different than passive Holdings
- Profound change in way we think about investment and also ownership
- Challenge of taxation around this
- A lot of wealth created in this space
- Bans push ownership to different jurisdiction
- Not really possible to control this
- NFT owners have different incentives than underlying asset owners; how to reconcile this?
- Piece of art called "Voice Gems"
- Environmental impact done on side chain
- minimize energy consumption

- other BC besides Ethereum, focused on minimizing environmental impact
- endangered species on "Voice Gems"
- Energy and computational challenges
- EV could be fractionally owned; looking at a specially Renewables
- Capital heavy items Fractionally owned
- Collaboration (decentralized) is the best way forward
- "A-jurisdictional" concept
- Convening Community is very important
- How do we work towards governance of BC's?
- Arresting climate change, altruism and Broader awareness
- Eth - eth 2.0
- Incentive for correct Behavior
- punitive for exceeding emissions or more voting power (carrot) for acting correctly
- Block ecosystem needs to pave the way
- Multi-stakeholder approach, can't have just governments or just the private sector moving us (hopefully quickly) and profoundly to better environmental situation
- ABT- Actor should come from large corporations to push this technology further
- Cryptokitties
- Video games – video clips of Slam Dunk
- Endangered voices on block chain

- Everything you buy now can be tokenized
- More voting power if acting in a more environmental way
- Everybody has to be involved in this
- Reward behavior
- NFT Artwork

Driving Circular Growth with Data

Yuki- Tohoku General HQ, The Yomiuri Shimbien
- 1.5 degree pathway
- For elements steel, cement, chemicals, aluminum
- Reduce emissions to Net Zero by 2050 - Circularity -2050
- AI, 3D printing
- Scale circular economy and net zero

The Honorable Hiroshi - Trade and Industry of Japan (METI)
- Promising digital technology lead to Global decarbonization
- 5G Telecom
- Green data centers realized
- Circular economy contribute greatly to Green economy
- A meta economy?
- 3R's- reduce, reuse, recycle
- Expand hydrogen uses - hydrogen and gas turbines in the Netherlands and USA

Shunichi - Mitsubishi Heavy Industries, Japan Circularity
- 3 R's, or use less, longer, smarter

- Useless material informatics, 3D printing, preventive maintenance, repair robots, partial repair 3D printing
- No single Pathway to NetZero or carbon neutral by 2050
- Expand hydrogen usage, hydrogen power gas turbines in Netherlands and US
- Hydrogen projects; green and turquoise iron oxide reduction by hydrogen in German steel works
- CCU- utilization long-term plan for decarbonization
- Utilize existing power plants, use ammonium instead of coal
- Advanced data collection
- Sophisticated control systems
- Increasingly distributed systems
- Advanced info systems, Quantum computing tracing of material and product history and circular economy
- Scrub handling and treatment process
- Shipping sector 3% of carbon emissions
- Cradle-to-cradle passport
- Identifying recycling options

Bo-Cerup - Maersk McKinney Moller Center, Denmark
- Decouple growth from emissions through use of digital technology
- 70000 ships with annual 300,000
- With data and tools, they will be able to monitor, set goals, track progress

- o Shipping part of much larger system much larger perspective needed
- o Needs standards and protocols in place
- o Partnerships are key enabler for shipping transition
- o What kind of Partnerships are needed?
- o Digital elements extremely important part of solution to Gathering data

Barbara - Ikea Retail (Ingka Group, Netherlands) www.ecare.com
- o Circular and climate positive by 2030
- o 1 billion people to live here
- o 60% Global emissions households
- o ⅓ energy consumption is made by households
- o Ikea follow green thread to select products that are sustainable (not more expensive than regular products from the sea
- o Circular hubs
- o Program to buy back furniture from consumers
- o Black Friday 2020
- o 39 million pieces of furniture repurposed in one year
- o Material research reduce climate footprint by 4.3% while sales increased by 6%
- o Technology is Major element driving improvement
    - o can track CO_2 reduction
    - o "what if" boards, AI driven

- o Through technology-enabled all stores to be distribution centers
- o With covid a would have needed 15 times more distribution centers
- o Using AI = economically positive and reduced admissions
- o Ikea sells home solar panels in 30 markets
- o Clean energy subscriptions
- o Helping all of us and ecosystems have more sustainable life

Gisbert - Klockmer & Co., Germany
- o collecting scrap
- o platform
- o disruptive tech

The Next Frontier: AR/VR

Sandra- Intel

Saeed- Smartworld
- o Augmented reality and virtual reality will play a big role in the future
- o Virtual trainings and Healthcare
- o Improve customer experience, try before by
- o Products with art 94 per cent higher conversion rate
- o Special VR version of Zoom

- Will brick-and-mortar exist in the future? Will still exist maybe for next 10 to 20 years; trend is to online at least for large retailers, There is an urge for people to go out
- So many have lost jobs, kids learning through Zoom based structure, covid accelerated adoption

Sly- Emerge
- Sense of touch, bonding important when not with them at this point in time
- People lonely, they seek deeper level of human connection
- Metaverse transaction
    - 2.0 shared media
    - 3.0 immersion
    - Emotion, info net
    - Convey emotion
- Look at social value, solve interpersonal connection new line connect with someone intimate moments, design Future tools, 70% Millennials feel lonely
- 79% gen Z and 61% are all lonely
- Sound pressure to create feel of objects midair
- AR / VR doesn't crack code on human connection and touch
- Touch is so important, no words to describe what we're going through

Judith- IMISI 3D from Nigeria
- African continent
- Arc V are all countries, all people

- Digital divide into convo
- XR extended reality
- Infrastructure critical
- 1.5 billion children out of school due to covid
- Electricity, internet
- Cannot purchase headset here
- If you're in a country where Amazon delivers you can have it shipped but it will cost double
- Africans could not afford it
- Options course correct Now
- LeapFrog

Go Global with Exar must include Africa and the rest of the world

Corporate Governance

Luis- The Inter. American Dev. Bank Bolivia
- 60% country has access to bandwidth, 20 to 50% of total income
- Infrastructure bill – access to connection
- Capacity of company to a naval technology across supply chains (for many and not the few)

Claire- Silicon Valley Bank
- Crowdfunding raise money
- Not as much regular technology
- Pandemic acute catalyst

- Goal is to inform, educate policymakers and support startups
- Check net bridging the valley, optimistic for infrastructure bill, sustained renewable energy
- Record IPOs in healthcare space

Amy- Salesforce
- Pandemic has done nothing but accelerate
- Championing higher taxes
- Disclosure more, rallying people around disclosure across Environmental/ ESG
- Focus on philanthropy 1%-time 1% product for charity 5,000 companies run off Salesforce platform for free investing in non-profit Community is critical

Christina- IBM
- Environmental & social statement
- Stakeholder capitalism
  - Unified framework around ESG metrics to provide more comparison
  - Disclose more YoY
  - What's important? Over the long-term
- Grassroots effort support charity
- Brooklyn

Todd-
Yale University

- o O&G create environmental challenges and enabling solutions beyond borders

Kay- Head of AI and machine learning/ WEF
- o Benefits maximized and risks mitigated
- o Center for 4ir

Facebook for free data - Now have Library
Concordia - controls Digital Money

3
Scriptural Basis About Digital Money in End-Time Scenario

When you understand the end-time scenario, it is abundantly clear how the digital money works with the mark of the beast and 666. First, we must understand the Lucifer is fake. He is UN-natural. He wants to set up his world in a fake digital utopia to where people will have to create loyalty to him through token. It is a "token" of appreciation. The "token" is through digital money.

In the beginning, God gave the first token. It was the promise to Noah that He will not destroy the Earth again with a flood. The token was a rainbow!

> *Genesis 9:13 I do set my bow in the cloud, and it shall be for a token of a covenant between me and the earth.*

God gave us that rainbow to promise us that He will remember what He has done and not do it again. It's His way of showing love to us. In the end, Lucifer is using the rainbow in a perverted way.

Token from Lucifer
Cryptocurrency   Rainbow currency
Noahide Laws!
The very thing that powers the ecosystem, RAINBOW token is a powerful 7 part token that brings a balance to the ecosystem. Pots of Gold.
https://rainbowtoken.finance/

Satan's crypto covenant   Crypt=death

TOKEN - a thing serving as a visible or tangible representation of a fact, quality, feeling, etc.

Definition of Crypto:
- Definition: a person having a secret allegiance to a political creed, especially communism

- crypto- a combining form meaning **"hidden," "secret,"** used in the formation of compound words: cryptograph. Also, especially before a vowel, crypt-[33]

---

[33] https://www.google.com/search?q=crypto+meaning&rlz=1C5CHFA_enUS945US945&oq=crypto+meaning&aqs=chrome..69i57j0i512l9.3577j1j7&sourceid=chrome&ie=UTF-8

Crypto & Bitcoin – Why Christians Must Not Participate

Definition of Crypt:[34]
- an underground room or vault beneath a church, used as a chapel or burial place.
- a small tubular gland, pit, or recess.

Definition of Token:

In general, a token is an object that represents something else, such as another object (either physical or virtual), or an abstract concept as, for example, a gift is sometimes referred to as a token of the giver's esteem for the recipient. In computers, there are a number of types of tokens.[35]

In the Bible it talks about a token given to us by God as a covenant that He will not flood the Earth again. It's a promise to us as His people.

---

[34] https://www.google.com/search?q=definition+of+crypt&rlz=1C5CHFA_enUS945US945&oq=definition+of+crypt+&aqs=chrome..69i57j0i512j0i10i22i30j0i22i30l4j0i10i22i30j0i22i30l2.9569j1j7&sourceid=chrome&ie=UTF-8

[35] https://whatis.techtarget.com/definition/token

It's like Lucifer is paying us back for what God did to him and his demons/giants back then.

Another way you can look at this covenant is the fact that it represents the natural. He said the covenant is between Him and the Earth. This is the natural covenant. The one Lucifer is creatig UN-natural covenant. Participate in his Metaverse and synthetic world with his tokens.

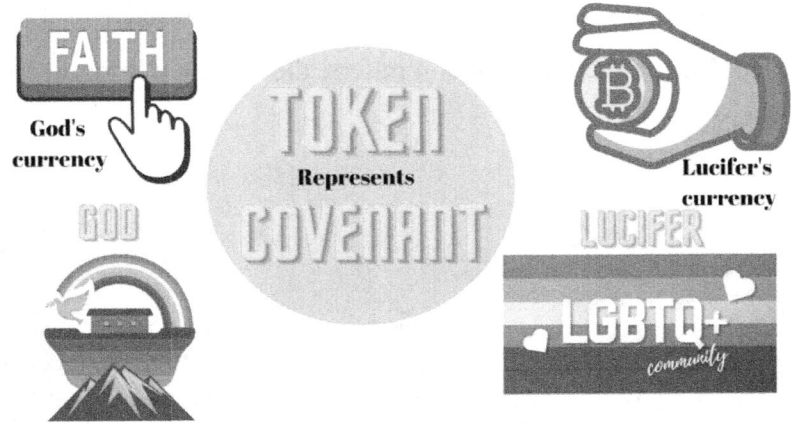

Look at this…

Crypto & Bitcoin – Why Christians Must Not Participate

- **Lion's Head**
- **Data Mining Tool**
- **Two fists holding up a T**
- **Hexagon Enclosure - 6 edges**
- **T is breaking UP the stone on the bottom - destroying foundation**
- **As above/So below with arrows**
- **Alister Crowley shape**
- **Double Tau**
- **Cup of his indignation**

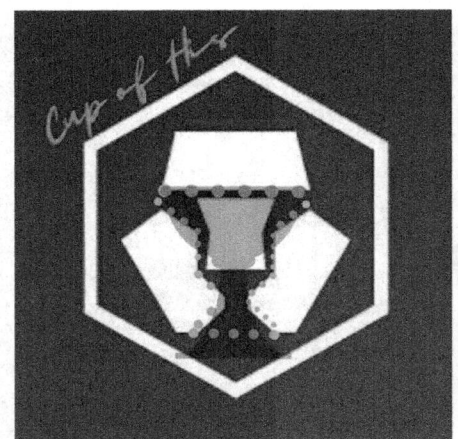

Crypto & Bitcoin – Why Christians Must Not Participate

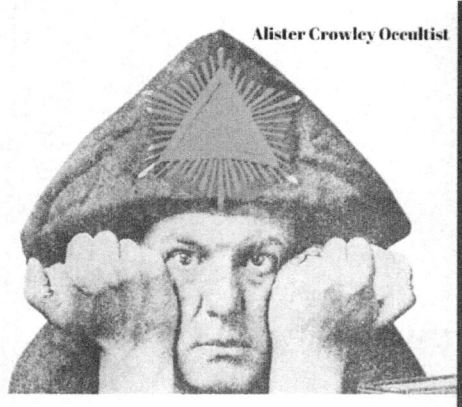

Crypto & Bitcoin – Why Christians Must Not Participate

As you can see by those pictures, the digital symbol is way too similar to Alister Crowley, a data-mining tool, the cup of indignation and a lion. The world that Lucifer is setting up right now is for the world to tell him everything. Put on your VR glasses and talk away. Express your wildest dreams in his world. Well, in order for you to be a part of this world, you will have to participate in the token economy.

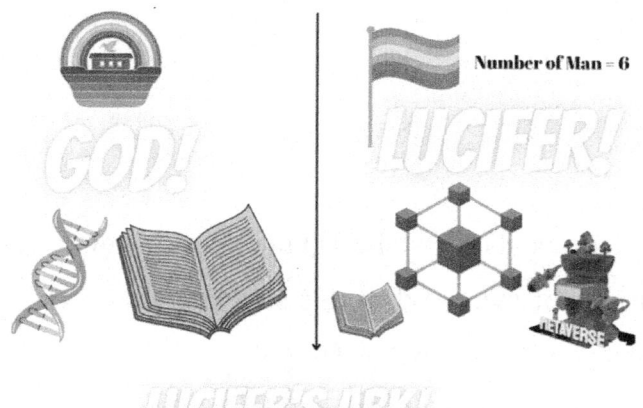

- **Metaverse**
- **Crypto-currency**
- **V & Digital ID System**
- **One World Order**
- **Digital Anything**

RAINBOW   **OLD & NEW**

- 6 color rainbow - LGBTQAI
- Rainbow Currency - Crypto - currency, Digital Money
- Rainbows & Unicorns (children)
- Rainbow in churches now (purple lights, pink, etc.)
- Rainbow clothing

In the world today they are using the rainbow in many ways.

The Bible describes the mark of the beast scenario as a way that we will not be able to buy or sell without this mark.

> *Revelation 13:17 - And that no man might buy or sell, save he that had the mark, or the name of the beast, or the number of his name.*

Lucifer's rainbow, the LBTQ one, is a six colored rainbow. Six is the number of men. When this scripture says name of the beast, I believe that is the Internet of Things (IoT). The number of his name is 666. This could also be the build back better campaign, which is global. 6uild 6ack 6etter. It could also be the code within the digital money.

The Mark of the Beast

Revelation 13:16 - And the second beast required all people small and great, rich and poor, free and slave, to receive a mark on their right hand or on their forehead, 17 so that no one could buy or sell unless he had the mark— the name of the beast or the number of its name. 18Here is a call for wisdom: Let the one who has insight calculate the number of the beast, for it is the number of a man, and that number is 666.

So, many people believe it's going to be a literal mark on the hand or forehead like this:

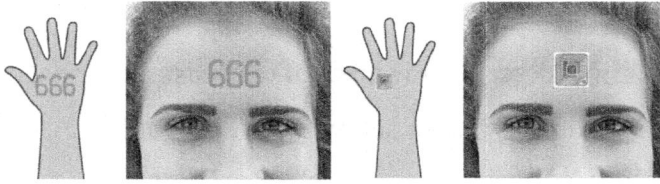

Right now, they are implementing global ID systems which will partner with the crypto system – the new digital system.

In this system, you will have your own key. This key will allow you to use currency in this economy.

We the People

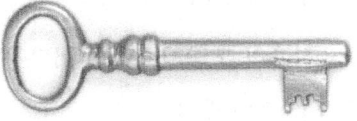

We the people is a lie saying that the people-centered design is the safest way for currency. They tell each person they will have control over their own money. Their unique key will be controlled by the human, and not some big bank or government.

To Round it Up:

Explaining the complicated aspect of cryptocurrency, uscybersecurity.net explains, "By definition, cryptocurrency represent any form of currency that only exists digitally. Cryptocurrency usually has no central issuing or regulating authority. In contrast, it uses a decentralized system to record transactions and manage the issuance of new units. That process relies on cryptography to prevent counterfeiting and fraudulent transactions.

If it is difficult to explain the concept itself, then it must be even harder to execute business successfully. Indeed, a lot of people are not willing to risk it, so they play it safe by investing in other types of assets."[36]

---

[36] https://www.uscybersecurity.net/cryptocurrency-6-potential-dangers/

When trying to explain cryptocurrency to someone is difficult. As I stated in the Preface, I'm not the expert at this, but I can speak about this as a spiritual aspect. Cryptocurrency is the Beast currency. We can never participate in this world currency because it involves us making an allegiance to the Beast. I know from participating in UN meetings, etc., that this world is being shaped around the vaccine. Look at this from one of my news shows:

Here are some other graphics I've done around cryptocurrency and this agenda:

Crypto & Bitcoin – Why Christians Must Not Participate

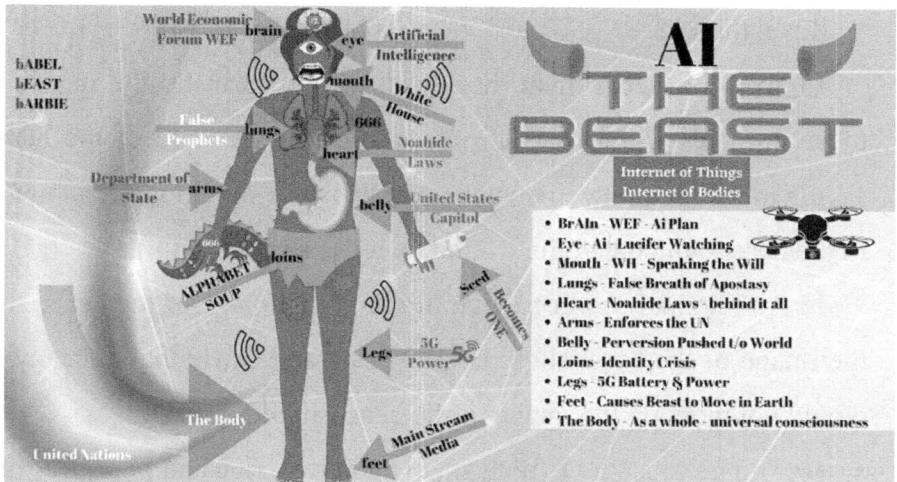

This above is my understanding of what's happening now. This is the big picture of the BEAST system. The picture below is the Microsoft 060606 patent that they did about six months before they rolled out the COVID agenda. You cannot make this stuff up! Basically, this patent says that it will reward the human by their obedience. This is the circular economy – a reward system.

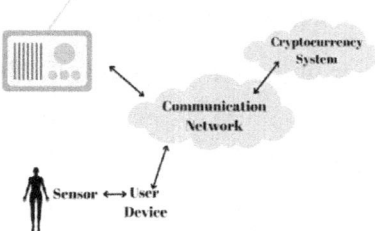

The token economy is part of the circular economy. It is a system of reincarnation. What goes around comes around. In this circular world, they want you relying on the Beast system for everything. Lucifer wants all eyes on you and your 100% loyalty. Also, think of this currency like a slave system.

Revelation 13 –

14 And deceiveth them that dwell on the earth by the means of those miracles which he had power to do in the sight of the beast; saying to them that dwell on the earth, that they should make an image to the beast, which had the wound by a sword, and did live.

15 And he had power to give life unto the image of the beast, that the image of the beast should both speak, and cause that as many as would not worship the image of the beast should be killed.

16 And he causeth all, both small and great, rich and poor, free and bond, to receive a mark in their right hand, or in their foreheads:

17 And that no man might buy or sell, save he that had the mark, or the name of the beast, or the number of his name.

18 Here is wisdom. Let him that hath understanding count the number of the beast: for it is the number of a man; and his number is Six hundred threescore and six.

I hope this book has helped you, Bride. It will at least give you more information to consider in the coming days. God bless.

ABOUT THE AUTHOR

We Are the Bride Ministries Founder

Dr. June Dawn Knight is a White House Correspondent, pastor, author, media specialist, mother, and grandmother. Her heart is to serve her community. She has been in public service for the last 25 years. She spearheaded four organizations. The Middle Tennessee Jr. League Cheerleader's Association in which she unified four different counties and ten cities for cheerleading. MTJLCA still exists today. She also served as the president of the Steelworker's Union for the CMCSS Bus Drivers in 2004/2005. Then, she went to World Harvest Bible College in Columbus, Ohio. Following Bible College, she attended APSU from 2008 – 2012. During her time at APSU, she spearheaded three organizations on campus. Dr. June Dawn served student life and served on the Provost Committee for the students.

Dr. June Dawn graduated APSU in December 2012 with her master's Degree in Corporate Communication. She studied in London during Grad School under the top three global Public Relations/Advertising Firms in the world. During this time under the instruction of the University of Kentucky, she made a 100 in the class. She graduated with a 3.74 GPA. Dr. June Dawn had dreams of traveling the world for a major corporation, however, after graduation, God stopped her plans and called her back to the ministry.

Through the years Dr. June, as she is fondly referred to, has spearheaded multiple organizations that bring people together and give them a platform; many of which continue to function today. Additionally, Dr. June has served in multiple ministries all over the world working alongside visionaries to assist them in clearly defining, articulating, and supporting implemental strategies that reflect and maximize the effectiveness of their Godly calling.

Currently as the CEO and president of WATB ministries, she has an astute ability to see through the deception that is unfolding in the world, along with an approach of reporting truth unlike any of our time. Her knowledge, experience and wit combined provide material that is godly, informative, and life-changing for so many across the globe.

From London to the White House, Dr. June has been on an extraordinary journey to discover the heart of the spiritual condition of the country. The Lord intertwined her within ministries all over to give her a birds-eye view of ministry in today's culture. As the Lord sent her to the White House, remains a representative of the true church on a global level. She has the global picture of the church's situation and condition with the Lord.

Through the years of suffering, traveling, and serving, Dr. June represented the Bride of Christ at the White House with truth and grace. The assignment there only lasted a year (the last year of America 2018-2019). Following this assignment, the Lord brought her back to Tennessee where she is now with her family.

From London to the White House. Now she writes books about what she has learned to help the Bride.

Dr. June's Education:

Bachelor's Degree in Public Relations at Austin Peay State University

Master's Degree in Corporate Communications at APSU. While in Graduate School at APSU, Dr. June studied in London (Winter 2011/2012) and studied under the top three global marketing/advertising/communication firms in the world. She wrote a 20-page research paper comparing how the United Kingdom markets a product versus the United States. Dr. June completed the class with a grade of 100! Following graduation, she turned that paper into her first book, *Mark of the Beast*.

- One year of studies at World Harvest Bible College
- Doctor of Theology at International Miracle Institute

Prior to this book, she has written 17 books. This is the eighth book of the *What the World?* Series. These books will help the Bride to understand the end-time events taking place and to prepare for Heaven.

Made in the USA
Middletown, DE
02 April 2022